W9-AXG-731

PLANET SOS

OUT OF ENERGY

Gerry Bailey

Gareth Stevens
Publishing

Library of Congress Cataloging-in-Publication Data

Bailey, Gerry.
 Out of energy / Gerry Bailey.
     p. cm. — (Planet SOS)
 Includes index.
 ISBN 978-1-4339-4978-4 (library binding)
 ISBN 978-1-4339-4979-1 (pbk.)
 ISBN 978-1-4339-4980-7 (6-pack)
 1. Power resources—Juvenile literature. 2. Renewable energy sources—Juvenile literature. I. Title.
 TJ163.23.B355 2011
 333.79—dc22

                                    2010032889

Published in 2011 by
Gareth Stevens Publishing
111 East 14th Street, Suite 349
New York, NY 10003

Copyright © Diverta Ltd. 2011
All Rights Reserved.

Designer: Simon Webb
Editor: Felicia Law

Printed in the United States of America

CPSIA compliance information: Batch #CW11GS: For further information contact Gareth Stevens, New York, New York at 1-800-542-2595.

CONTENTS

WHAT IS ENERGY?

Scientists explain energy as the ability to do work. It's the ability of something to move something else a specific distance. Every time you move, you use energy, and you get that energy from food. Everything that moves or grows needs energy, and just as you eat different kinds of food, so there are lots of different sources of energy in the world.

Kinds of energy

There are two basic kinds of energy: kinetic energy and potential energy. Kinetic energy is the energy of motion. It's the energy an object has when it is moving, such as a bicycle, a train, a ball, or your legs! Potential energy is stored energy. Chemical energy, nuclear energy, and electrical energy stored in a battery are all kinds of potential energy.

When we use energy it doesn't disappear. It just changes into a different kind, or kinds, of energy, and the total amount of energy always stays the same. The energy from electricity, for example, can be turned into heat energy.

A battery contains stored, or potential, energy.

4

The ball has kinetic energy, or energy of movement, and so do these runners.

Natural resources

Natural resources often have potential, or stored, energy. And the Earth provides us with plenty of natural resources that we use as fuel to produce other kinds of energy. The natural resource that we've been using a lot of in modern times is called fossil fuel. Fossil fuels include coal, petroleum (crude oil) and natural gas.

Fossil fuels were formed millions of years ago from buried plants and tiny animals. They contain chemical energy that is a form of potential energy. Burning fossil fuels to produce heat or electricity releases millions of tons of carbon dioxide into the atmosphere each year.

Unfortunately, carbon dioxide is a greenhouse gas, collecting in the atmosphere and contributing to global warming. So we have to look to other, cleaner natural resources to provide our energy, such as the sun, wind, rivers, and oceans.

FOSSIL FUELS

Coal is a fossil fuel that's been used by humans over many hundreds of years. In much of the world it used to be the main fuel for heating homes, but today it's largely used by industry and in power stations to produce electricity.

It takes millions of years to create coal. It's a sedimentary rock that's composed mostly of carbon and hydrocarbons. The energy in coal comes from the energy stored in trees and plants that died hundreds of millions of years ago. They were part of the swampy forests that covered the Earth at that time. When the forests died they made a layer at the bottom of the swamps and in time were covered over with layers of soil and water. Over millions of years, heat and pressure turned the forests into coal.

How coal forms

Over millions of years, plants that died in swamps were covered with water and soil.

Heat and pressure from above turned the plant material into coal.

The environment

Unfortunately, when we burn coal we release unwanted materials into the atmosphere. These include carbon dioxide, or CO_2, the number one greenhouse gas, as well as sulphur dioxide and nitrogen oxides, which cause acid rain. Scientists have discovered three main ways of reducing the damage that is caused by these gases. One way is to clean the coal after it is mined and before it goes into the furnaces. Another process uses equipment called scrubbers to clean the sulphur from the smoke before it leaves the chimney. A third possible method is called carbon capture. The CO_2 is removed and pumped into storage underground, where it can be kept permanently.

Oil shortage: gas-guzzlers

Oil, like coal, is a nonrenewable energy source. That means quite simply that when we run out, there's none left.

Oil started as plants and tiny animals that lived in water 300 to 400 million years ago. Over millions of years, the remains of these animals were covered in sand and silt. Heat and pressure gradually turned them into oil, or petroleum. So the oil we use today cannot possibly be replaced before we have used up all of Earth's supply.

Oil has been used as a fuel, or energy source, for thousands of years. But when mass production of cars began at the beginning of the 20th century, oil was turned into gasoline to fuel them. Gasoline is now the main oil product.

At a refinery, crude oil is broken down into gasoline, diesel, and other products.

So much oil is used to fuel cars that it is shortening the time before oil reserves run out.

A smaller car helps the environment and may help our oil reserves last a little longer.

Gas-guzzlers

Gas-guzzlers are big cars that use a lot more gas to travel the same distance as smaller cars. Gas-guzzlers are considered to be environmentally unfriendly, not just because they use up so much gas, but because by burning more gas they create more of the greenhouse gas emissions that scientists believe are responsible for increased global warming. Other emissions can include sulphur dioxide, which makes acid rain, nitrogen oxides, and particulates that can harm health.

Governments are trying to persuade people to buy smaller cars by adding a heavy tax to the price of gas. What should persuade us is knowledge of the damage we are doing to the environment by driving gas-guzzlers when we don't need to.

Oil spills

When oil spills happen they can cause terrible damage to the environment. We've all seen pictures of seabirds or other sea creatures that can no longer fly or swim because they're covered in slimy crude oil. Oil spills can also harm humans by affecting, for example, fishing and tourism. Oil spills used to be mainly the result of oil tankers becoming involved in accidents at sea.

That happens less frequently now, as new tankers are required to have a double hull lining to protect against spills. But they still happen because of oil pipeline leakage.

Deepwater Horizon

On April 20, 2010, a massive explosion shook the oil rig Deepwater Horizon located in the Gulf of Mexico. The explosion caused thousands of barrels of oil a day to gush into the sea from a broken pipe on the ocean floor. The oil began to drift towards the coast of the United States. On April 22, the Deepwater Horizon sank. Scientists studying video footage of the oil billowing out of the pipe say that up to 100,000 barrels could be leaking into the sea – every day.

Wild birds will die if their feathers are not cleaned of oil.

Chemical dispersant

One way of dealing with oil spills is to treat them with a chemical dispersant that breaks up the oil. But many of these are themselves toxic, or poisonous, and could be dangerous to sea life, especially in deep water.

The thick red oil slick from Deepwater Horizon coats the coastal beaches and wetlands of Louisiana. Volunteers work to clean it up.

RENEWABLE ENERGY

We can't go on using fossil fuels once they're gone, so we have to find alternatives. Already, we are finding ways to harness some of Earth's natural sources of energy, such as sunlight, wind, waves, and tides. There are other sources too. Geothermal energy uses the natural heat below Earth's surface. Or we can generate energy from biomass, which is organic material such as crops, manure, and some kinds of trash – it's a renewable energy source because we can replace it by raising more animals and growing more trees and crops. And one thing's for sure – there will always be waste to get rid of, and so much of what we throw away can still be useful to us.

Waste not, want not

When organic waste is thrown away, it rots, decomposes, and releases methane gas into the atmosphere. By lining the landfill site and covering the trash with a thick membrane, it's possible to collect the methane so that it can be used as a fuel. It can be treated and sold as a fuel for cars or burned to make steam and electricity.

Organic waste in landfills produces billions of tons of methane gas.

Experts think that in Europe alone, landfill sites could yield billions of cubic yards of methane each year, but currently only 1 percent of this is being collected.

There are many other ways of producing energy that don't exhaust the planet's resources and don't damage the environment by polluting the atmosphere, and more are being discovered all the time.

This spectacular building in Vienna, Austria, houses a giant incinerator that burns trash. This heat, together with excess heat from nearby factories, is then used to provide hot water and heating for local homes, as well as to generate electricity.

Solar energy

The sun has been a source of energy ever since it began its life billions of years ago. Called solar energy, it comes in the form of waves, which can be converted into other kinds of energy such as heat or electricity. When it's converted to heat, known as thermal energy, it's used to heat water for homes, offices, and swimming pools. It can also be used to heat spaces such as the inside of homes, factories, and greenhouses. The great thing about solar energy is that it doesn't directly produce air or water pollution.

Sunshine is called radiant energy because it moves in the form of electromagnetic waves, or rays.

Thermal solar panels

Thermal solar panels absorb and collect the sun's radiation. This energy is usually used to heat a liquid that can then be pumped through a building to provide hot water and heating. Solar panels are made up of a dark-colored absorber that absorbs the solar energy (heat), a transparent cover, and a heat transporter, generally water or a mix of water and other liquids, that flows through tubes from the absorber and into the plumbing system.

Photovoltaic cells

A photovoltaic (PV) cell is used to convert solar energy into electricity. It's made of silicon alloys. As well as waves, sunlight can be seen as particles of energy called photons. When photons hit a PV cell, some are absorbed by it. They provide the energy to create electricity by making the surfaces of the cell act like the negative and positive terminals of a battery. When the surfaces are connected through an appliance, electricity flows. Electricity produced in this way is "clean" energy – emitting no greenhouse gases or other pollution.

Rooftop thermal panels provide hot water.

To boost power, photovoltaic cells are connected together in modules to form an array.

Solar cybercafe

Not everyone in the world has easy access to computers or to the Internet, something many of us take for granted. Computer Aid International, an IT (information technology) charity, shipped more than 170,000 recycled computers to the developing world. And now they have launched something a bit different.

Internet in a box

Take an old shipping container, insulate it, furnish it with electric lighting, desks, chairs and personal computers, and you have the makings of a cybercafe, or Internet café, that can be taken anywhere in the world. All you need is electricity, because there are many places in the world where there is no available power. The answer is to install a roof-mounted photovoltaic array. Now you have a solar-powered cybercafe!

Solar power and the computer

These solar arrays are only powerful enough to run one computer. And a cybercafe needs more than that. So a system was chosen that allowed the use of one computer, a Pentium 4 PC, that could be split out into ten workstations. Because there's only one computer to power, the PV panels can also power a light and recharge cell phones.

A single computer works like a server and is split out so that ten people can use workstations.

An old shipping container becomes a solar-powered cybercafe.

Wind energy

Wind is the movement of our atmosphere, or air. The air above warmer areas expands and rises. At the same time cooler air blows in to take its place, making wind. The energy from this moving air can be captured and used to generate power. Usually wind energy is used to make electricity. It's a clean fuel, producing no pollution as nothing is burned to create power.

Wind turbines

Wind turbines work just like the windmills that were used to grind wheat into flour. They use blades that turn when the wind blows over them and creates lift. The blades are connected to a drive shaft that turns an electric generator to make electricity.

Another kind of wind turbine is called a vertical axis turbine. It looks a bit like an egg beater, with blades that stretch from the top to the bottom.

It takes a great many wind turbines to produce a reasonable amount of electricity, so they are often built in groups, called wind farms. Wind farms are sited on rounded hills, open plains, and shorelines. Many wind farms have been placed offshore as well.

The kite-surfers are using wind power to pull themselves along in the water.

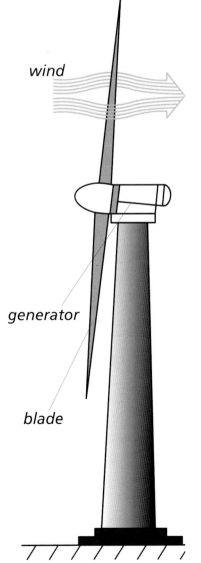

As the wind passes round the blade, it creates lift. This forces the blade to spin. A generator inside turns mechanical energy into electrical energy.

wind

generator

blade

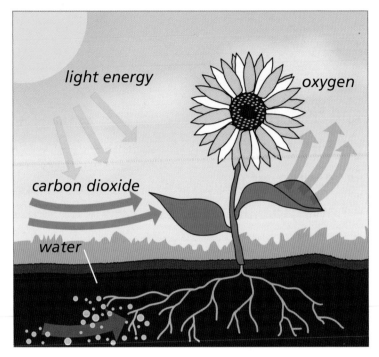

Photosynthesis is the process plants use to get energy to grow and reproduce.

Biomass

Biomass is plant and animal material. Plants store the sun's energy via photosynthesis, the process through which they convert sunlight into chemical energy in the form of sugars. This gets passed on to animals, including humans, when the plants are eaten.

Biomass materials include waste products from industry, such as sawdust and wood chips from a timber yard. These can be turned into pellets and used to fuel electricity generation.

This power plant burns waste wood to generate electricity.

Biodiesel

Biodiesel is a type of diesel fuel oil that is made from vegetable oils such as soy and rapeseed and new crops such as camelina that have a high oil content. Biodiesel can also be made by reprocessing used cooking oil, which is collected from restaurants and then filtered and refined. Biodiesel can be added to conventional diesel fuel and used in vehicles.

This bus runs on soy biodiesel, a renewable fuel.

Ethanol 85 can be used in most gas powered cars.

Bioethanol

Bioethanol is an alcohol made by fermenting the sugar components of plant materials, and it is made mostly from sugar and starch crops including sugar beet, wheat, sorghum, corn, and sugarcane. Ethanol can be used as a fuel for vehicles in its pure form, but it is usually used as an additive to increase performance and improve vehicle emissions.

HYDROPOWER

Hydropower is energy that comes from moving water. It is another renewable energy source that relies on a natural phenomenon that is always taking place – the water cycle. When the sun heats water on Earth, the water evaporates into water vapor. This condenses into clouds and falls back to Earth as rain or snow. This water eventually flows through rivers back to the sea, where it evaporates and begins the cycle all over again.

Hydroelectric energy

The water that flows along a river can have a lot of energy, especially if it is moving quickly or if it's falling from a height in the form of a waterfall.

As the Niagara River plunges over the falls, some of its water is funneled off to generate electricity.

Stop the flow

Sometimes the natural flow of a river is used to produce energy, while at other times a dam is built to store water in a reservoir.

This dam is holding back the water, creating an artificial lake.

Turn the turbine

The water used to create electrical energy is passed through a pipe called a penstock. The rushing water hits turbine blades that spin a generator to produce electricity.

Rushing water hits the blades of a turbine that turns a generator.

Nearly clean

Although using the flow of water to create energy provides a clean energy source, it can have negative effects on the environment. A reservoir and dam may change the temperature, chemistry, and silt loads of the river, which may affect plants and animals. Large-scale engineering works can also affect farms and whole villages, which may even end up being submerged. Careful management of the water resource is needed.

The generator creates electricity that's sent to the power company.

Tidal power

Tides are caused by a combination of the rotation of Earth and the gravitational pull of the moon and the sun. The sun has only about a third of the power of the moon to cause tides because it is so far away. Using the movement of water caused by the tides is called tidal power or tidal energy. Tidal energy is useful because it's more predictable than wind or solar energy.

Tidal barrage

One way of harnessing the energy from the tides is to build a dam, called a barrage, across a coastal inlet. The area inshore of the dam is called a tidal basin. Sluice gates control the flow of water, allowing water to flow into the tidal basin when the tide comes in. Some systems use a turbine system on both the in and the out movements of the sea to generate electricity.

The barrage system at La Rance in France is one of the few barrage systems in the world.

The Severn Bore is a tidal surge that happens in the spring on the River Severn in England. There are plans to harness its energy with a tidal turbine.

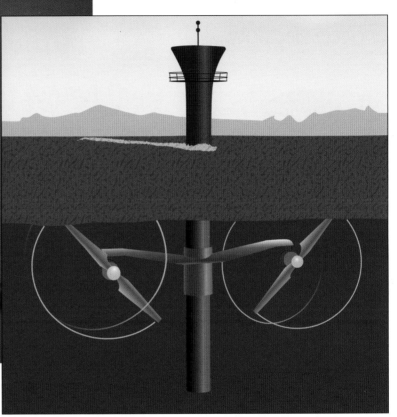

The fast-flowing tides at Strangford Lough in Northern Ireland are used to propel this tidal turbine.

Tidal turbines

Another way of harnessing tidal energy is by setting up tidal turbines. Tidal turbines work in the same way as wind turbines. They have blades that are turned by tidal movement. The blades are attached by a drive shaft to a generator. But because water is so much denser than air, tidal turbines have to be a lot stronger than wind ones and are more costly to build.

GEOTHERMAL ENERGY

Geothermal energy is heat that comes from inside Earth. The word "geothermal" comes from two Greek words, *geo* meaning Earth and *therme* meaning heat. Because Earth produces heat all the time, geothermal energy is renewable. We can capture Earth's heat as steam or hot water and use it to heat buildings or create electricity.

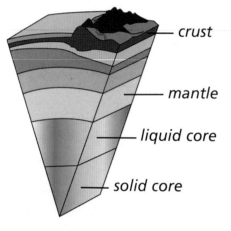

— crust

— mantle

— liquid core

— solid core

Cross-section of Earth's layers.

Heat below the ground

Earth's core is very hot – even hotter than the surface of the sun. Above the core lie the inner and outer mantles. The outer layer, the crust, is just 15.5 to 34 miles (25 to 55 km) thick on the continents. The crust is not a single solid layer, but is made up of pieces called plates. Geothermal heat usually bursts through where these plates meet.

Geothermal reservoirs

Areas where there are natural heat resources under the ground are known as geothermal reservoirs. Mostly they are very deep down and geologists can't always tell where they are, although they may drill a well and test the temperature. However, sometimes geothermal energy comes to the surface in the form of volcanoes, hot springs, and geysers.

Plants such as this one convert geothermal energy to electric energy.

Using the energy

Geothermal power plants produce electricity. They're usually built above a geothermal reservoir that's just a few miles below ground. Wells are drilled and hot water is piped to the surface, where it's converted to steam to turn the generator turbines.

Sometimes geothermal energy is piped directly from its source. It is delivered directly into buildings to heat them. It can also be used in industry and agriculture.

Almost all the buildings in Reykjavik, Iceland, use geothermal heating.

NUCLEAR ENERGY

An atom is a tiny particle made up of a number of electrons that move around a nucleus. Everything in the universe is made up of atoms. They're so small that a grain of sand contains millions of them. But the bonds that hold the atom together contain huge amounts of energy. This energy can be released by either splitting the atom, which is called nuclear fission, or combining it with another atom, which is called nuclear fusion. Nuclear power plants use nuclear fission to produce electricity.

Fission energy

Nuclear fission happens when a small particle called a neutron hits a uranium atom and splits it into two parts. This releases a large amount of energy in the form of heat and radiation. High-speed neutrons are released when the uranium atom is split, and they go on to hit and split more atoms in a chain reaction.

1. A neutron is fired at great speed towards a uranium atom.

2. The neutron splits the atom in two.

3. A huge amount of energy is released

4. Neutrons from the split atom hit more atoms, in a chain reaction.

Nuclear reactors

Nuclear plants use uranium that's formed into pellets about the size of a pea. They're placed end to end in metal fuel rods. A bundle of these rods is called an assembly, and a reactor core, where fission takes place, is made up of a number of assemblies. Water is pumped into the reactor. Fission in the reactor heats the water.

This heated water is kept under pressure and it heats a second supply of water to produce steam. The steam turns turbine blades that drive an electric generator to produce electricity.

The nuclear reaction makes so much heat that cooling towers are needed, like the ones above.

Radioactive downside

Radioactivity is very dangerous. Some people don't like the idea of nuclear power plants because if anything goes wrong, such as an uncontrolled nuclear reaction, there's a chance that radioactivity might contaminate the air and water around the plant. This could damage the health of people living nearby. There is also the problem of what to do with used reactor fuel, as it can remain radioactive for thousands of years. It's usually stored deep underground in concrete or steel containers.

Drums of nuclear waste are marked with an internationally recognized sign to warn of dangerous radiation.

HYDROGEN

There is more hydrogen in the universe than any other gas. Stars such as the sun are made mostly of hydrogen. It's the simplest element, with just one proton and one neutron in its atom. Hydrogen is so light it rises through the atmosphere and into space, so we don't find any hydrogen gas naturally on Earth. It is, however, found in compounds with other elements. Water is made up of hydrogen combined with oxygen. Hydrogen combined with carbon can form methane.

We can use hydrogen as a fuel or an energy carrier, like electricity. Energy carriers move energy from one place to another. But first the hydrogen must be separated from the other elements it is mixed with.

Making hydrogen

Hydrogen can be made using two methods: steam reforming and electrolysis. Steam reforming separates hydrogen atoms from carbon atoms in methane. But this process causes greenhouse gas emissions. Electrolysis is more expensive but doesn't produce harmful emissions.

Uses of hydrogen

Hydrogen is used in industry but it's also used as a fuel. NASA uses liquid hydrogen to propel space shuttles into orbit. Hydrogen batteries, called fuel cells, create electricity to power the shuttle's electrical system. The process leaves water as a by-product, which the crew then uses as drinking water.

Hydrogen powers the space shuttle into orbit.

Hydrogen fuel cells

Hydrogen fuel cells are used to produce electricity. They work by combining hydrogen and oxygen gases. When these gases combine they produce

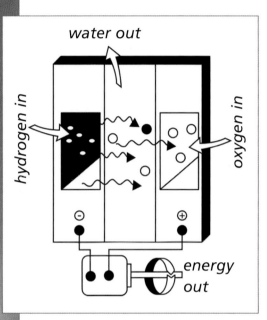

water, electricity, and heat. The electricity can then be used to power engines. There are no polluting chemicals produced.

So far fuel cells are too expensive to be used generally. A network of refuelling stations

would be needed and these don't exist at the present time. However, many people believe that hydrogen could be the fuel of the future.

In many cities around the world,
hydrogen-powered buses are being used.

X PRIZE

Some of the most important inventions and advances in history have been the result of winning a competition. The X PRIZE is a competition offering a $10 million prize to produce a car with a super-efficient, nonpolluting engine. This is the Aptera, one of the competition entries. It is battery-powered and has a top speed of 84 miles (135 km) per hour.

PEDAL POWER

People can actually be a source of energy. We use human energy to get from one place to another when we pedal a bicycle. Another use for people power is the treadle pump. A treadle pump uses human energy to lift water from just below ground level through a tube well. The pumped water can then be used to irrigate fields. Water can also be drawn in this way from rivers or lakes.

The treadle pump fills irrigation channels that carry water to the crops.

Out of poverty

Farmers in the north Indian plains used to rely on the monsoon rains, which meant they could raise just one crop each year. Now they use treadle pumps to irrigate their fields and can grow three or four crops per year. In the past, some family members would have to leave home to work in the cities for part of the year, but now families can stay together and farm all year and earn a cash income from their produce.

Charity pumps

A charity working in India called IDEI has helped spread the use of treadle pumps by organizing a network of manufacturers, retailers, and installers. So far more than half a million pumps have been manufactured and sold in India and more than a million in Bangladesh.

A woman works the treadle pump, causing water to flow to the fields.

Treadle pumps

A treadle pump uses a kind of lever that's pressed by the foot. Power comes from the operator's muscles and body weight. The lever drives two pistons that create cylinder suction to draw water to the surface. A treadle pump can lift 176 to 247 cu feet (5 to 7 cu m) of water per hour from a well.

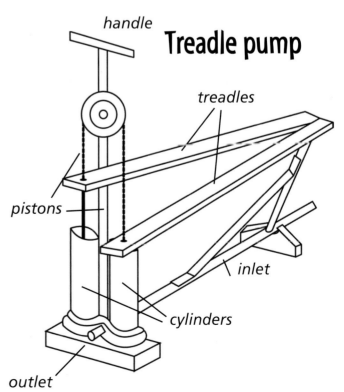

Treadle pump

handle

treadles

pistons

cylinders

inlet

outlet

City of bikes

Many cities in Europe were built long before cars were invented. So in some places the streets are too narrow for most vehicles to drive through. Parked cars can block the flow of traffic so cars are not welcome. Amsterdam in the Netherlands is an example. But its citizens have helped solve the problem by riding bicycles instead of driving cars. Many other cities could reduce pollution as well as congestion if they encouraged the use of bikes.

Amsterdam is an old city with narrow streets and many canals.

Perfect for cyclists

Amsterdam is both flat and small, so it's the perfect place for cyclists. And nearly everyone in Amsterdam owns their own bike. The city has its own bicycle coordinator whose job it is to make sure biking is always safe, easy, and encouraged. There is a huge network of safe bicycle routes and secure bike sheds. Almost half of all traffic movement in the city is by bicycle.

If you are visiting the city you can rent a bike quite easily. You will be an environmentally friendly guest. And you'll use up 400 calories per hour by pedaling compared to 58 calories per hour going by car.

In Amsterdam, it's usual to ride your bike to work.

Many other cities could reduce pollution and congestion if they encouraged the use of bikes.

HOT AND COLD

We waste a lot of the heat energy from our homes and workplaces because it escapes into the atmosphere. Half the heat loss in a typical house is through the walls and roof. To stop heat escaping we need to use insulation, which prevents heat from passing through walls, ceilings, and floors.

Ways to insulate

There are different ways to insulate a building properly. Thick blankets called quilts, made of soft materials such as fiberglass, are usually used. They are fitted between roof beams. A more environmentally friendly material is sheep's wool. It makes an excellent insulator.

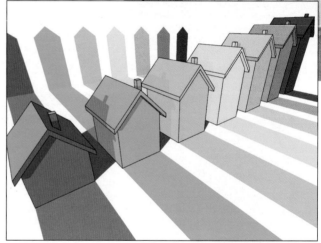

In some countries, houses are scored on how insulation efficient they are. The dark green house has the highest score and the red house the lowest.

Draft proofing

Draft proofing is one of the least expensive but most efficient ways to save energy in your home. It involves blocking unwanted gaps that let out warm air and let in cold air. This reduces the energy you need to heat the area. Chimneys and fireplaces can cause drafts as well as badly fitting floorboards and skirting boards.

Insulation can save energy – and money.

Rooms in the ice hotel aren't heated – except by people's body warmth.

Too hot

In hot countries many modern buildings have air-conditioning. This works like a combination of a refrigerator and a powerful fan. The warm air inside the building is sucked into the processing unit, where the temperature is reduced, then the cooled air is blown back into circulation.

Air-conditioning uses a lot of electricity, so it's expensive. It also uses energy that has probably been made from fossil fuels. Architects who design new buildings are looking for systems that are less wasteful. One is ice-cooling, which uses nighttime electricity, when demand and prices are lower, to freeze large tanks of water into ice. In the daytime, air is blown over the ice and circulated through the building's ventilation ducts.

Keeping heat out

Twenty years ago a company in Sweden built the world's first ice hotel from blocks of ice and snow. Today there are ice hotels in many other cold countries too. In the ice buildings the only heat comes from the body warmth of the guests, and the average air temperature is between 17 and 23°F (-5 and -8°C).

CARBON FOOTPRINTS

A carbon footprint isn't actually a footprint. But it acts like one. It tells you how much CO_2 you leave behind you, or have used, just as a footprint leaves a mark.

Every household and each one of us leaves behind a carbon footprint made up of the amount of emissions we create individually or at home, school or work. It's calculated as the weight of CO_2 you use each year in tons.

Personal footprint

Lots of things make up your carbon footprint; you can't control them all, but you can do your part to help reduce your footprint and slow down global warming.

There's the energy you use at home for light and heat as well as everything electrical. A four-bedroom house with oil-fired central heating and around 25 lightbulbs will emit about 8.3 tons (7.5 metric tons) of CO_2 per year, depending on all the electrical gadgets and appliances that you use.

Then there's the energy you use when you go anywhere. Cars and planes add to your carbon footprint because of the CO_2 that their engines discharge into the atmosphere. Trains and buses do too, but because these are shared forms of transport, your individual emissions are less when you use them.

Estimate your carbon footprint

Your carbon footprint is a measurement of how your lifestyle affects carbon emissions. You can make a difference in it by making small changes in your everyday life. It's really just about being a little more thoughtful about the way we use energy. Many countries have Web sites to help you work this out and there's a list at:

www.oneplanetvision.org/individuals/footprint-calculators/

HELPING HAND

Most cars run on fossil fuels, and we know that fossil fuels are running out. They're not renewable and when they're gone, that's it – they're gone!

This may not be such a bad thing because when fossil fuels release their energy, like in a car engine, they emit carbon dioxide into the atmosphere, where it contributes to the greenhouse effect and global warming. Car manufacturers are developing new kinds of car engines, but meanwhile we all need to reduce our carbon footprint.

We must all learn to use our cars less

- Use a car only when it's really necessary.
- Share car rides whenever possible.
- Buy energy-efficient cars that use less gas.
- Tires that are properly inflated use less gas.

Reduce your carbon footprint

If you walk or bike to school instead of traveling by car, you will not be using any form of fuel – just your own energy! You will be helping to reduce the amount of fuel consumption on the planet. You will be reducing YOUR carbon footprint – the amount of gas emissions for which YOU are responsible.

Install a micro wind turbine

If you live in an area where there is plenty of wind, your family could install a "micro" wind or "small wind" turbine to power your home. A mast-mounted turbine is freestanding and can be put up where there is the most wind. The output is around 2.5 to 6 kilowatts. Roof-mounted turbines are smaller, generating 1 to 2 kilowatts, and can be erected on the roof of your house.

Use solar panels

Install solar thermal panels and you can heat up water for your showers and your radiators. Install solar PV panels on your roof and you can generate your own electricity. You can save around a ton of CO_2 per year as well as reducing electricity bills.

Turn it off!

If you leave televisions, stereos, and computers on standby, they are still on and using energy. Turn them off! And when your cell phone is fully charged, unplug the charger or it will keep using power.

GLOSSARY

acid rain Rain that is corrosive because it has absorbed harmful gas emissions from fossil fuels.

additive Something added to improve or enhance something.

air-conditioning A ventilation system that keeps the atmosphere cool and dry.

Aptera A prototype high-performance electric car.

atmosphere The layer of air surrounding Earth.

atom The basic unit of all matter.

barrage An artificial barrier at the mouth of a tidal estuary.

barrel A measure of volume in the oil industry. One barrel equals approximately 42 gallons (159 L).

biodiesel Diesel fuel made from vegetable oil.

bioethanol Ethanol (alcohol) produced by fermenting crops and used as a transport fuel, usually as an additive.

biomass Animal waste and plant materials used as a renewable energy source.

carbon A common chemical element that is abundant on Earth.

carbon capture A process of trapping CO_2 and pumping it into storage tanks (usually underground).

carbon dioxide / CO_2 A gas made of carbon and oxygen that is formed whenever carbon is burned. CO_2 is a major greenhouse gas.

carbon footprint A measure of the greenhouse gases that are produced by someone's actions and lifestyle as a result of burning fossil fuels.

chemical dispersant A chemical used to break up concentrations of organic material, such as spilled oil, at sea or in fresh water.

chemical energy Energy that is released or absorbed during the course of a chemical reaction.

core (of Earth) The center of Earth, composed of extremely hot iron.

crude oil Oil extracted from the ground but not usable as a fuel until it is refined. Also called petroleum.

cybercafe A public place, often a café, that provides access to the Internet.

dam An artificial barrier constructed across a river, often to create a reservoir.

Deepwater Horizon A semi-submersible offshore drilling rig that sank following an explosion in 2010.

diesel A petroleum-based fuel.

double hull A technique of shipbuilding in which two complete layers of watertight hull protect the ship from breaking open in a collision or accident.

emission Something that is emitted, or discharged, such as the exhaust from a vehicle or a chimney.

ethanol Pure alcohol, used in laboratories and as a fuel.

fiberglass A material made of fine glass fibers woven into a cloth and held together by plastic or resin.

fossil fuel Any fuel such as oil, gas, or coal that derives from the organic remains of past life preserved in rocks in Earth's crust.

fuel cell A device in which a fuel, such as hydrogen gas, is combined with oxygen to produce electricity, water, and heat.

generator An engine that converts mechanical energy into electrical energy.

geologist A scientist who studies geology – the history of Earth as recorded in rocks.

geothermal Relating to the natural heat that is below Earth's surface.

geyser A natural hot spring. Underground steam frequently throws up jets of hot water and mud.

global warming An increase in Earth's average temperature large enough to cause climate change.

gravity The force of attraction that pulls everything towards Earth's center.

greenhouse gas Any gas in Earth's atmosphere that traps heat and contributes to the greenhouse effect, including water vapor, carbon dioxide, and methane.

hydrocarbon An organic compound of carbon and hyrdogen often found in petroleum, coal, and methane. It is formed from organic matter that rotted millions of years ago.

hydroelectricity   Electricity produced by waterpower.

hydrogen   A colorless and odorless gas that is the lightest and most abundant element in the universe.

hydropower   Power derived from the force of moving water.

ice-cooling   A system of air-conditioning in which air is blown across blocks of ice.

incinerator   A furnace, usually for the destruction of garbage or other waste materials.

insulation   Use of materials to reduce the rate at which heat is absorbed or lost.

kinetic energy   The energy of motion.

kite-surfing   A sport that uses wind to pull a rider across the water on a small surfboard.

landfill   A garbage dump where domestic and commercial waste materials are disposed of.

manure   Animal waste and other organic matter used as organic fertilizer in agriculture.

methane   A powerful greenhouse gas, formed when organic matter rots. It can be used as fuel.

micro wind turbine   A miniature wind turbine that can be used to provide some of the electricity needed for private domestic use.

natural gas   A mixture of gases, consisting mostly of methane.

neutron   A particle forming part of the nucleus (center) of an atom.

nitrogen oxide   A gas formed of nitrogen and oxygen, which pollutes the atmosphere.

nuclear energy   The energy released by a nuclear reaction.

nuclear fission   A nuclear reaction in which the nucleus (center) of an atom splits into smaller parts, creating a huge amount of energy.

nucleus   The positively charged dense center of an atom.

oil rig   The platform and machinery for drilling a well to extract oil.

organic waste   Discarded plant and animal material largely composed of food waste.

pellets (wood)   A type of biomass fuel, generally made from compacted sawdust.

petroleum   See crude oil.

photon   A particle of electromagnetic radiation.

photosynthesis   The chemical process by which plants capture the sun's energy.

photovoltaic   Generating electricity directly from sunlight.

pollution   The contamination of the environment.

potential energy   Stored energy, such as that found in a charged battery, a wound-up clockwork motor, or a stretched rubber band.

radioactivity   Radiation emitted when atoms are split during a nuclear reaction, dangerous to living tissue.

refinery   An industrial plant in which crude substances (e.g. crude oil) are purified.

scrubber   A device in a chimney that removes particles and some polluting gases

sedimentary rock   A type of rock created over millions of years by the compression of sediment.

silicon   An abundant element used to make many things, including photovoltaic cells.

sluice   A man-made channel generally used to divert some water from the main flow.

solar energy   Energy emitted by the sun, or power obtained by harnessing that energy.

sulphur dioxide   A colorless gas that causes acid rain.

thermal energy   Energy in the form of heat.

tidal power   Energy that is derived from the difference in tidal levels.

treadle pump   A simple foot-operated pump ideally suited to basic irrigation.

turbine   An engine that uses a constant flow of air or liquid to spin something around.

uranium   A heavy radioactive metallic element used in the nuclear industry.

ventilation   Replacing stuffy air with fresh air.

wind farm   A group of wind turbines in the same location.

INDEX

PHOTO CREDITS

(t=top, b=bottom, l=left, r=right)